This Journal Belongs to:

_____

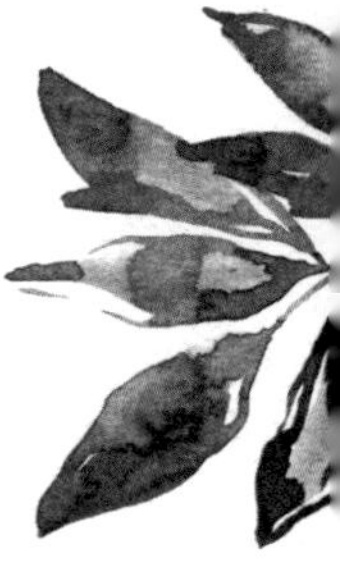

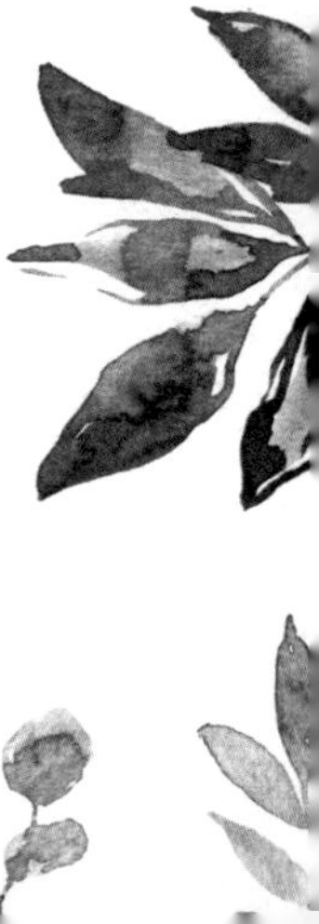

The best way to capture moments is to pay attention. This is how we cultivate mindfulness.

JON KABAT-ZINN

> The art of peaceful living comes down to living compassionately and wisely.
>
> —ALLAN LOKOS

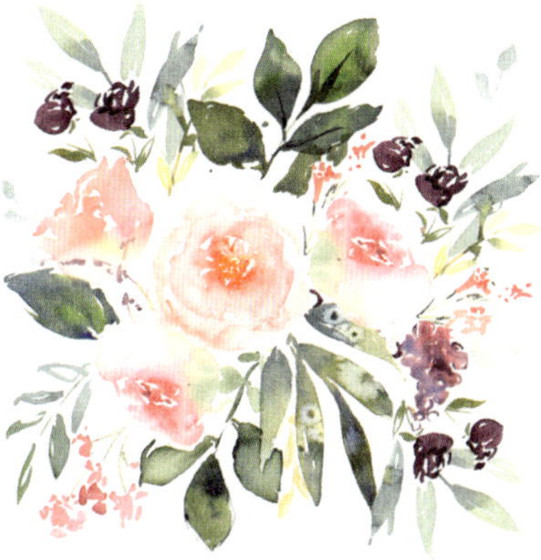

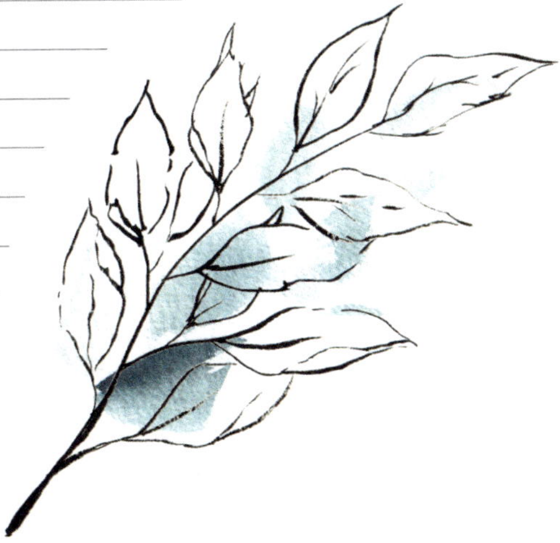

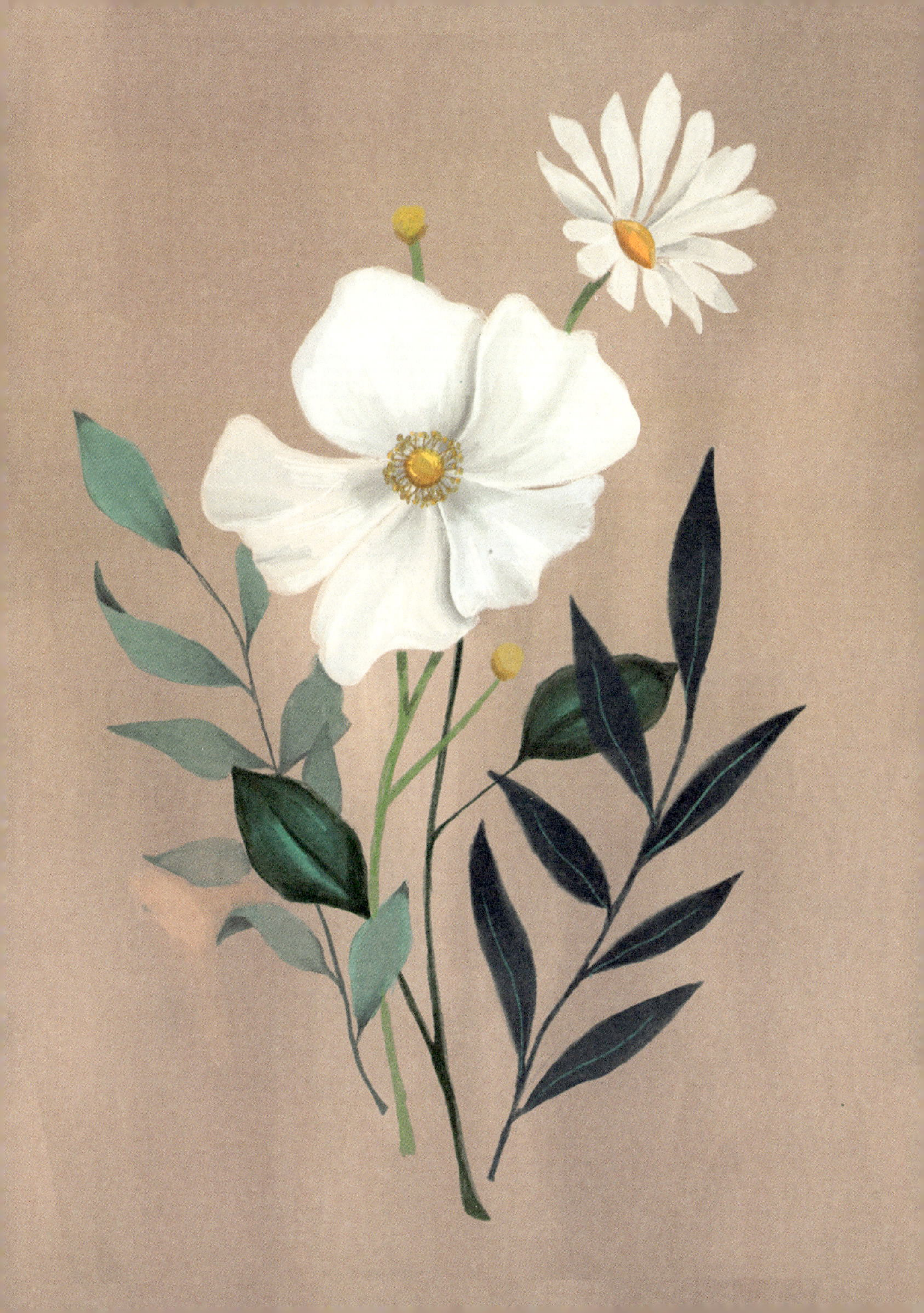

> *Be still,*
> *Stillness reveals the secrets of eternity.*
>
> — LAO TZU

Enjoy some quiet time before you rush into the world. Fluff a pillow. Pet a pet. Read a poem. Water a plant. Watch the steam rise from your coffee or tea. All of this chosen peace will serve as a powerful prayer for more peace. It will represent your request to the universe for calm and clarity in your day.

KAREN SALMANSOHN

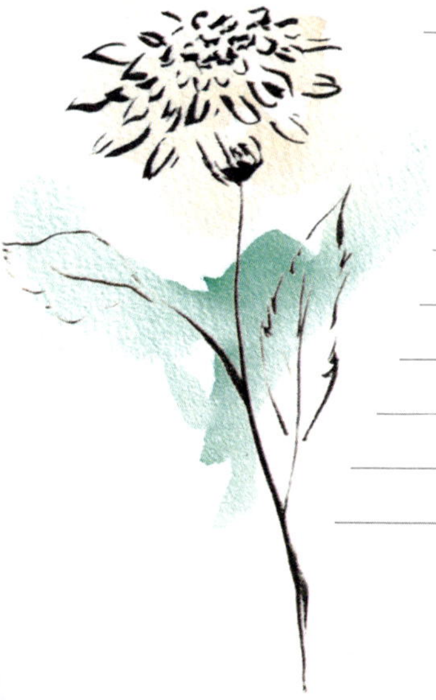

If you feel lost, disappointed, hesitant, or weak, return to yourself, to who you are, here and now and when you get there, you will discover yourself, like a lotus flower in full bloom, even in a muddy pond, beautiful and strong.

MASARU EMOTO, *THE SECRET LIFE OF WATER*

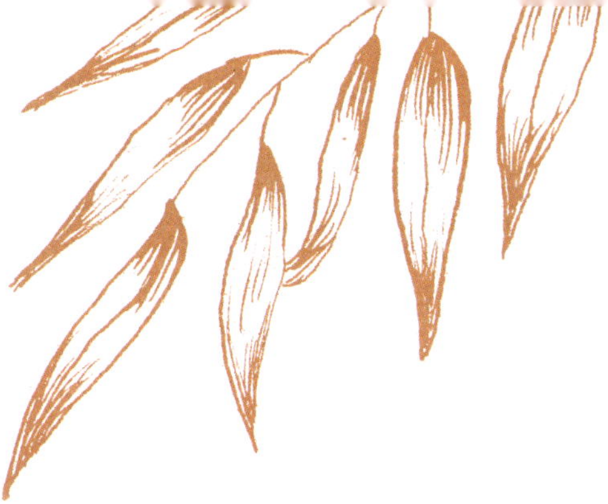

Authenticity is the daily practice of letting go of who we think we're supposed to be and embracing who we are.

BRENÉ BROWN,
THE GIFTS OF IMPERFECTION

Life is a collection of moments. Mindfulness is beautification of the moments.

AMIT RAY, *MINDFULNESS*

EVERYTHING THAT HAS A BEGINNING HAS AN ENDING. MAKE YOUR PEACE WITH THAT AND ALL WILL BE WELL.

Jack Kornfield,
BUDDHA'S LITTLE INSTRUCTION BOOK

Compassion is not complete if it does not include oneself.

ALLAN LOKOS,
PATIENCE: THE ART OF PEACEFUL LIVING

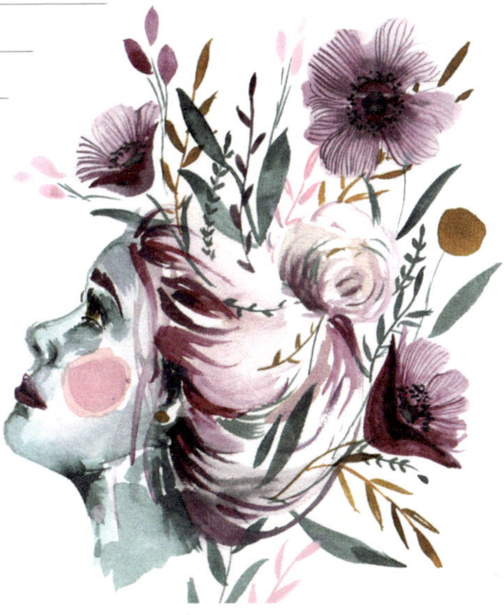

ALWAYS HOLD FAST TO THE PRESENT. EVERY SITUATION—INDEED EVERY MOMENT—IS OF INFINITE VALUE
FOR IT IS THE REPRESENTATIVE OF A WHOLE ETERNITY.

Johann Wolfgang von Goethe

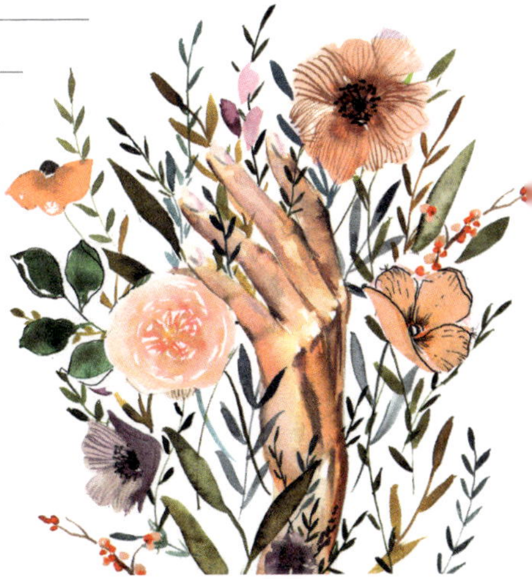

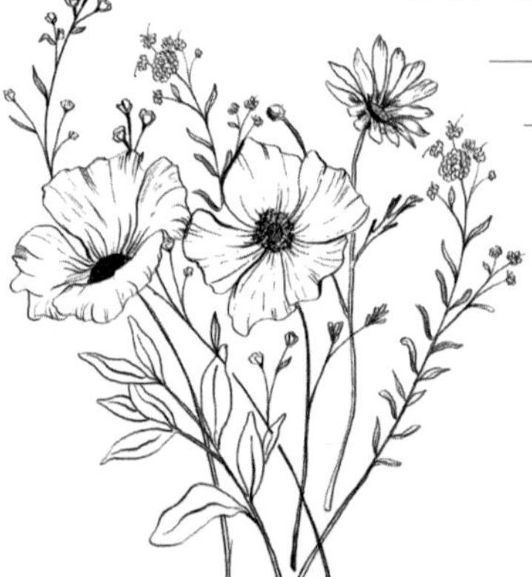

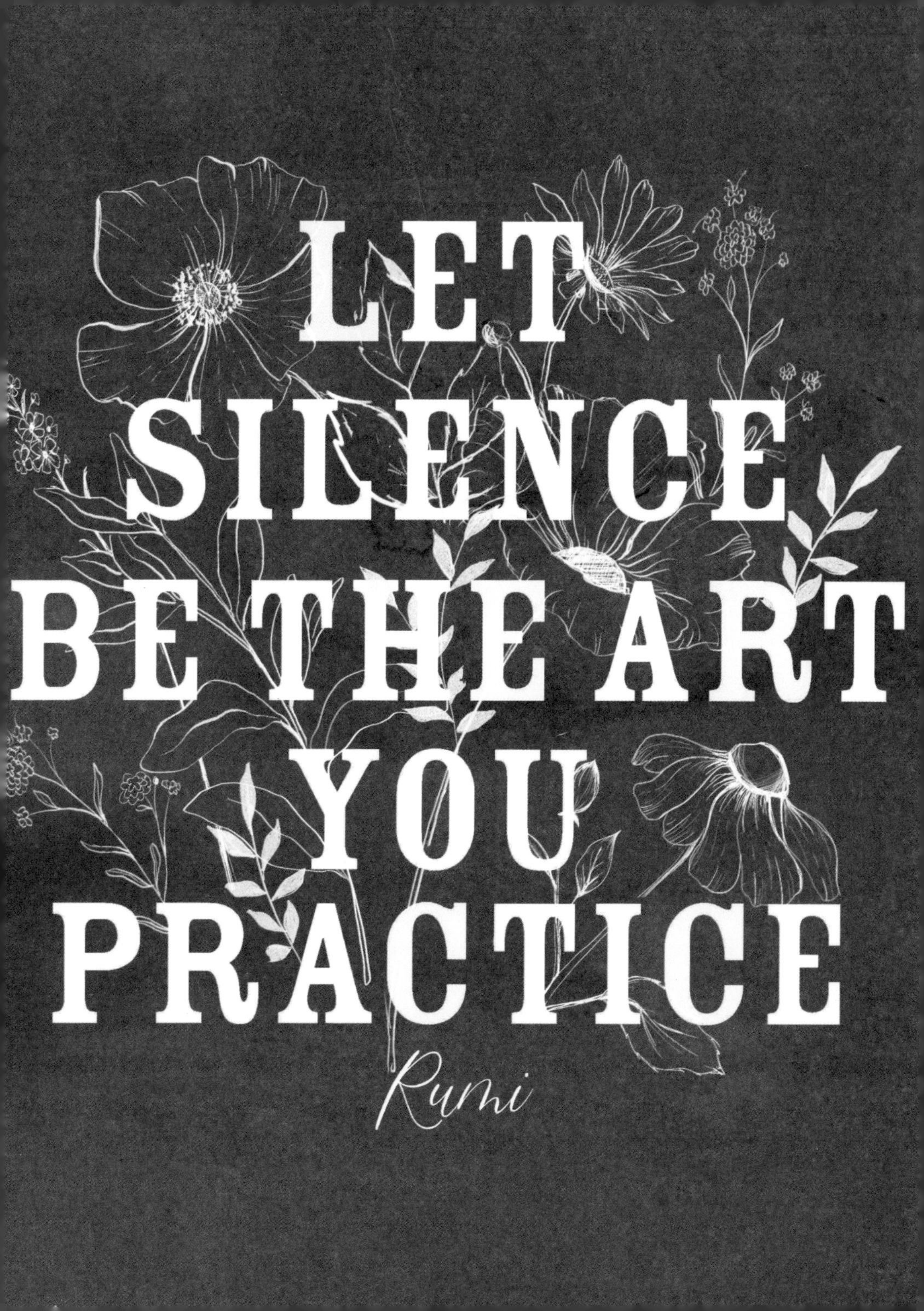
LET
SILENCE
BE THE ART
YOU
PRACTICE
Rumi

The ideal of calm exists in a sitting cat.

— JULES RENARD

> THIS IS THE REAL SECRET OF LIFE—TO BE COMPLETELY ENGAGED WITH WHAT YOU ARE DOING IN THE HERE AND NOW. AND INSTEAD OF CALLING IT WORK, REALIZE IT IS PLAY.
>
> ALAN WATTS

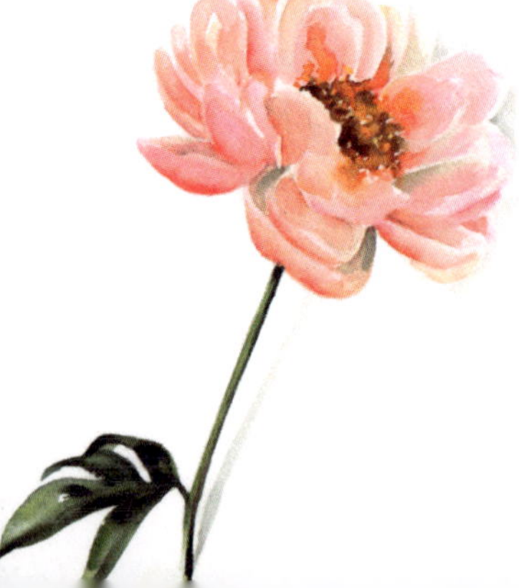

THERE IS A VOICE THAT DOESN'T USE WORDS. LISTEN.

WHAT YOU FEED YOUR MIND,

LEADS YOUR LIFE.

Kemi Sogunle

The present moment

is the only

time over which

we have dominion.

THICH NHAT HANH,
THE MIRACLE OF MINDFULNESS

There are a thousand reasons to live this life, every one of them sufficient.

MARILYNNE ROBINSON, *GILEAD*

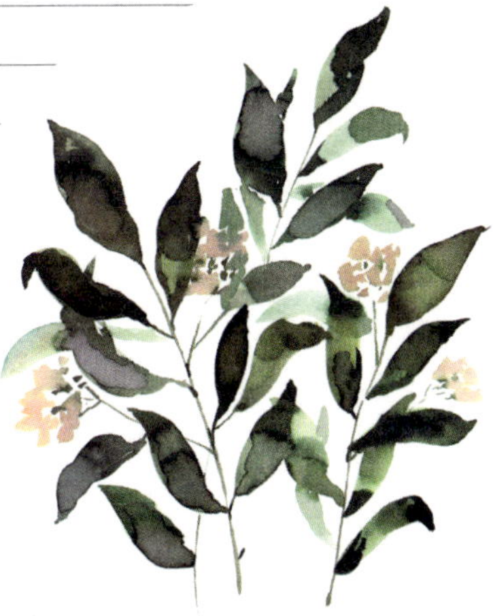

When we create peace and harmony and balance in our mind, we will find it in our lives.

LOUISE HAY

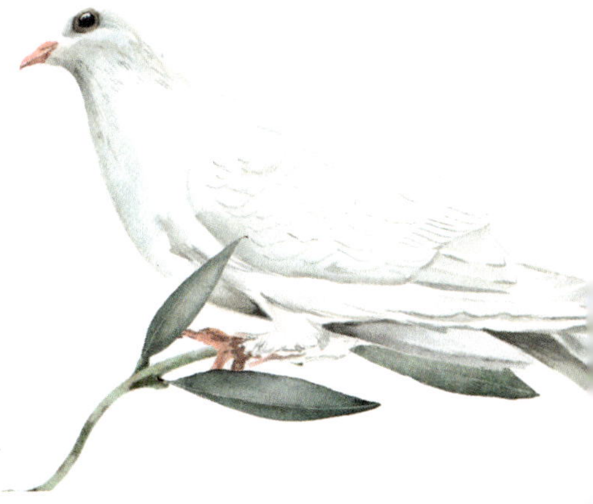

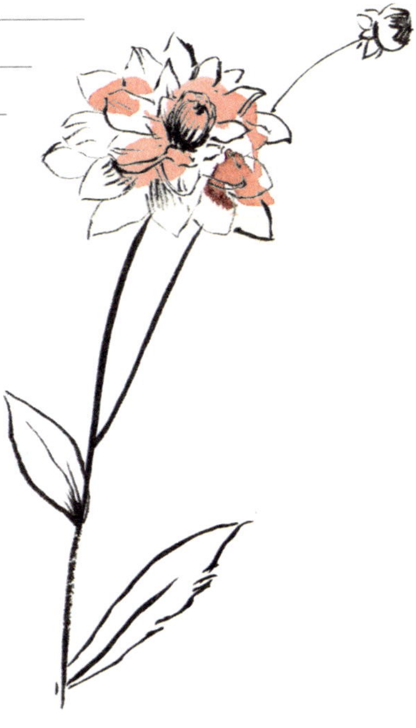

The most precious gift we can offer others is our presence. When our mindfulness embraces those we love, they will bloom like flowers.

THICH NHAT HANH

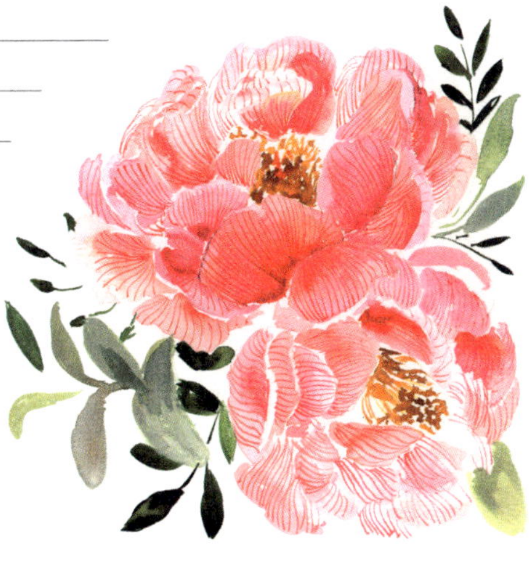

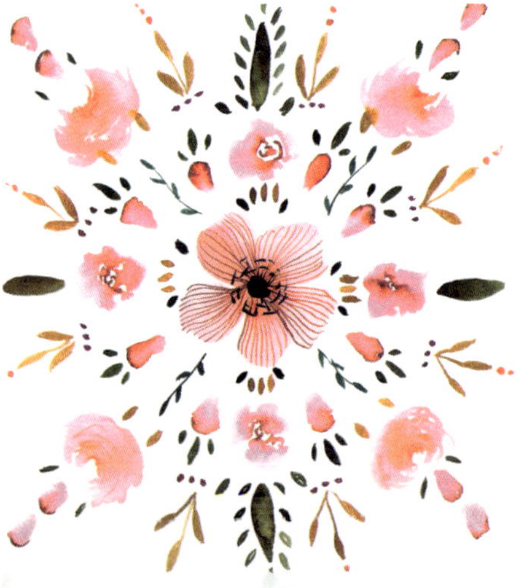

*You find peace
not by rearranging the
circumstances of your life,
but by realizing
who you are
at the deepest level.*

ECKHART TOLLE

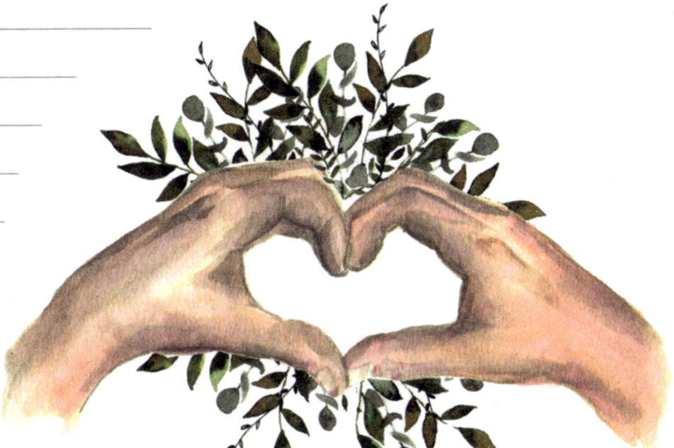

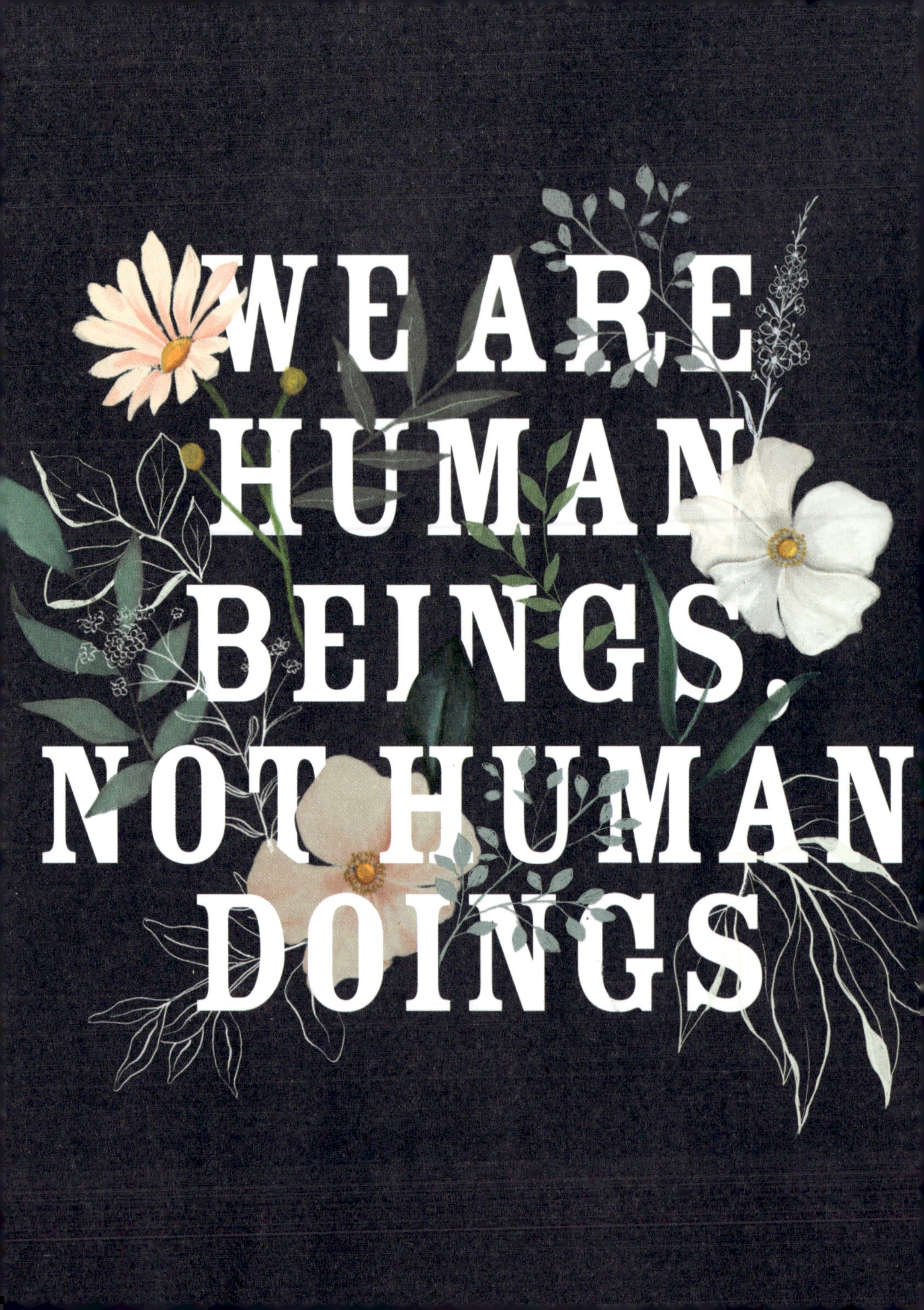
WE ARE
HUMAN
BEINGS,
NOT HUMAN
DOINGS

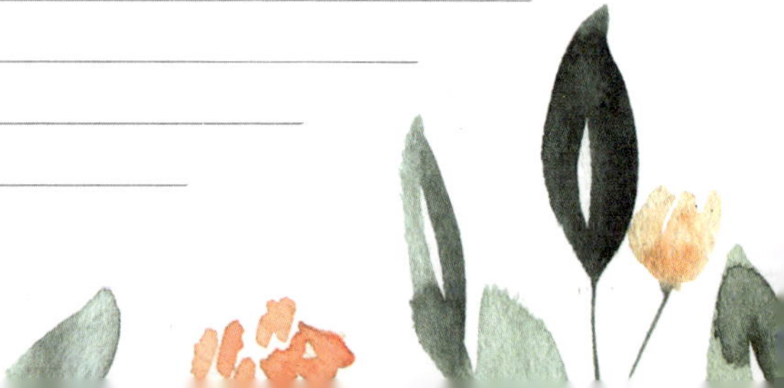

QUIET THE MIND AND THE SOUL WILL SPEAK.

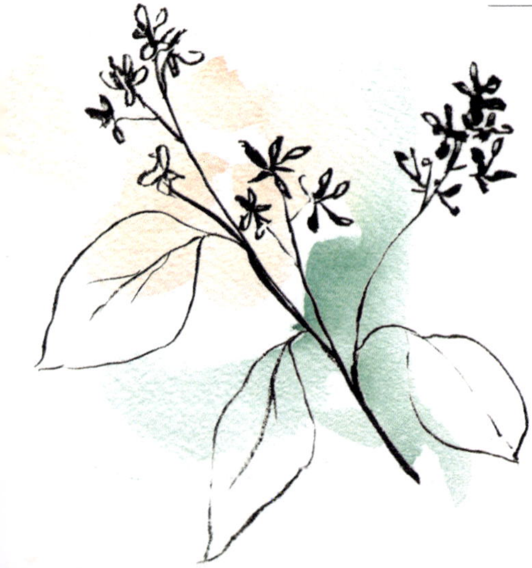

Many people are alive but don't touch the miracle of being alive.

— THICH NHAT HANH

*Every experience,
no matter how bad it seems,
holds within it
a blessing of some kind.
The goal is to find it.*

GAUTAMA BUDDHA

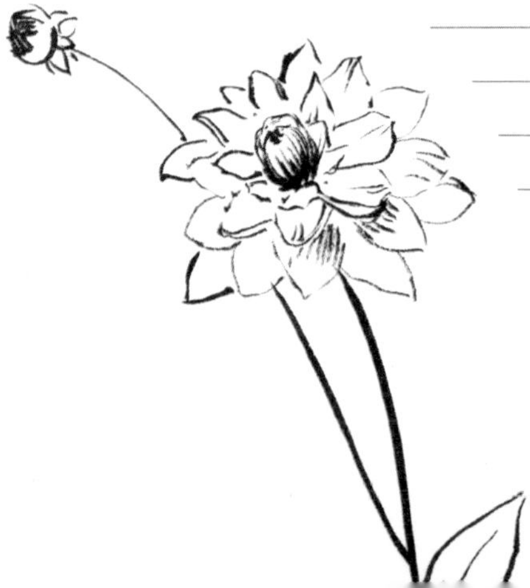

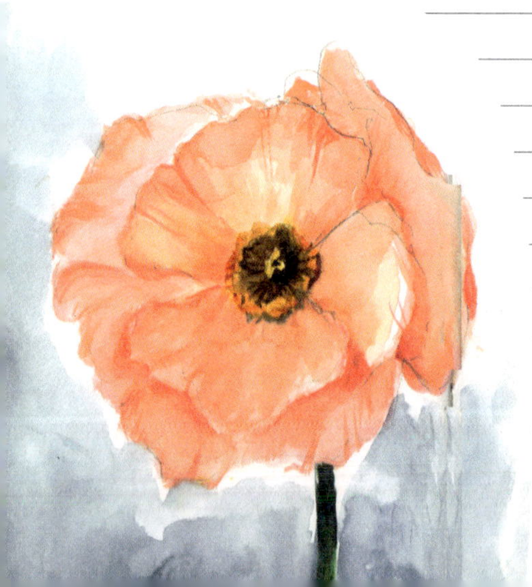

WHEN YOU
REALIZE NOTHING
IS LACKING,
THE WHOLE WORLD
BELONGS TO YOU.

Lao Tzu

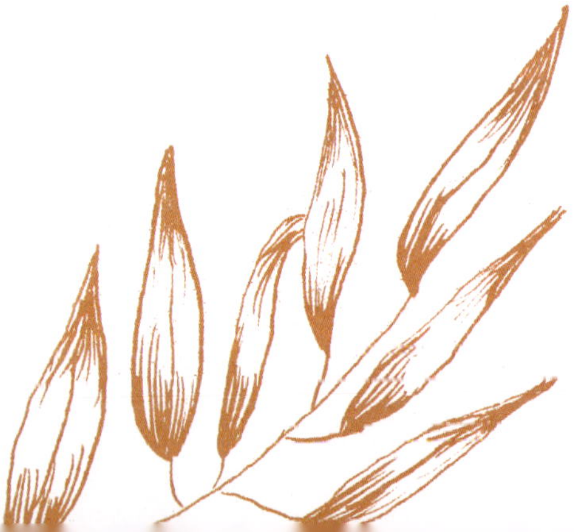

There is something

wonderfully bold and liberating

about saying yes

to our entire

imperfect and messy life.

TARA BRACH

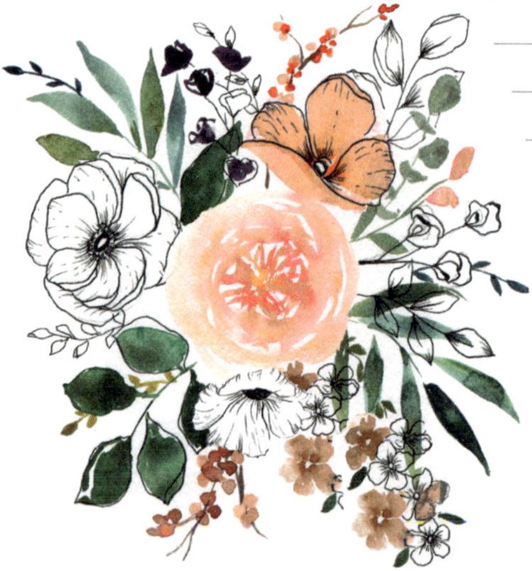

WHATEVER THE PRESENT MOMENT CONTAINS,
ACCEPT IT AS IF YOU HAD CHOSEN IT.
ALWAYS WORK WITH IT, NOT AGAINST IT.

Eckhart Tolle

DON'T SEARCH FOR ANYTHING EXCEPT PEACE. TRY TO CALM THE MIND. EVERYTHING ELSE WILL COME ON ITS OWN.

Baba Hari Dass

Within you there is a stillness

and a sanctuary

to which you can retreat at

any time and be yourself.

HERMANN HESSE, *SIDDARTHA*

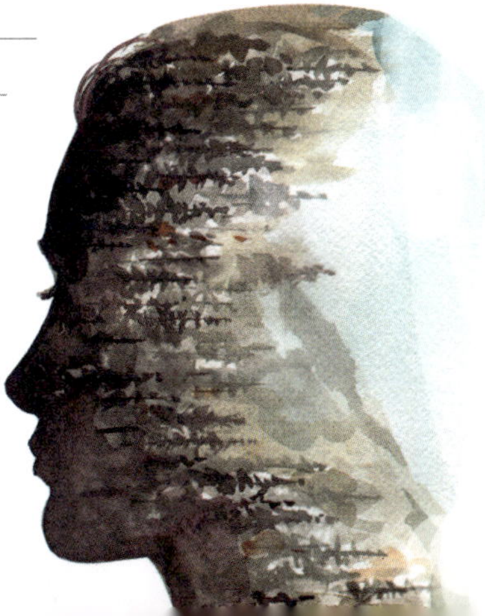

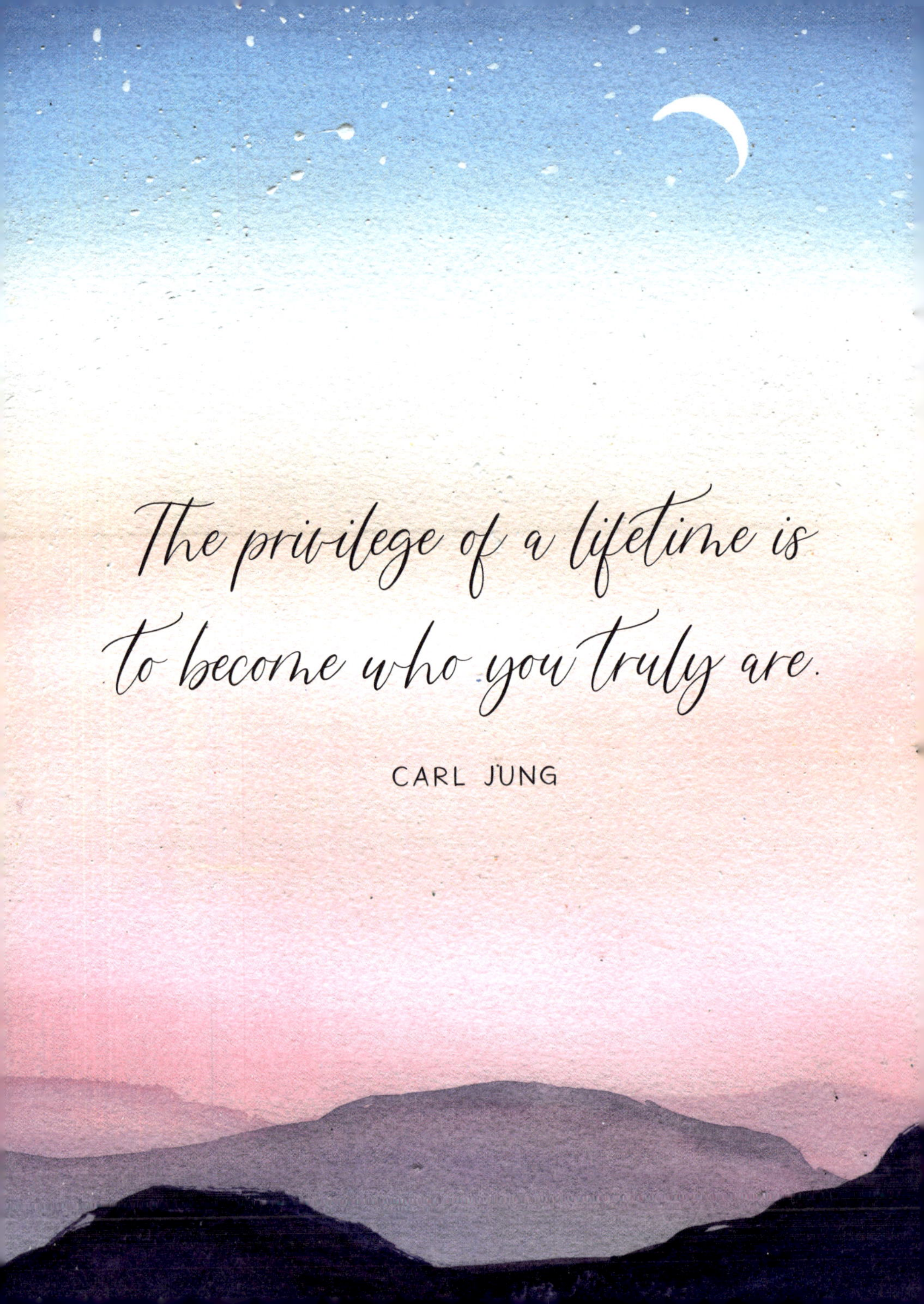
The privilege of a lifetime is
to become who you truly are.
CARL JUNG

The feeling that any task is a nuisance will soon disappear if it is done in mindfulness.

— THICH NHAT HANH

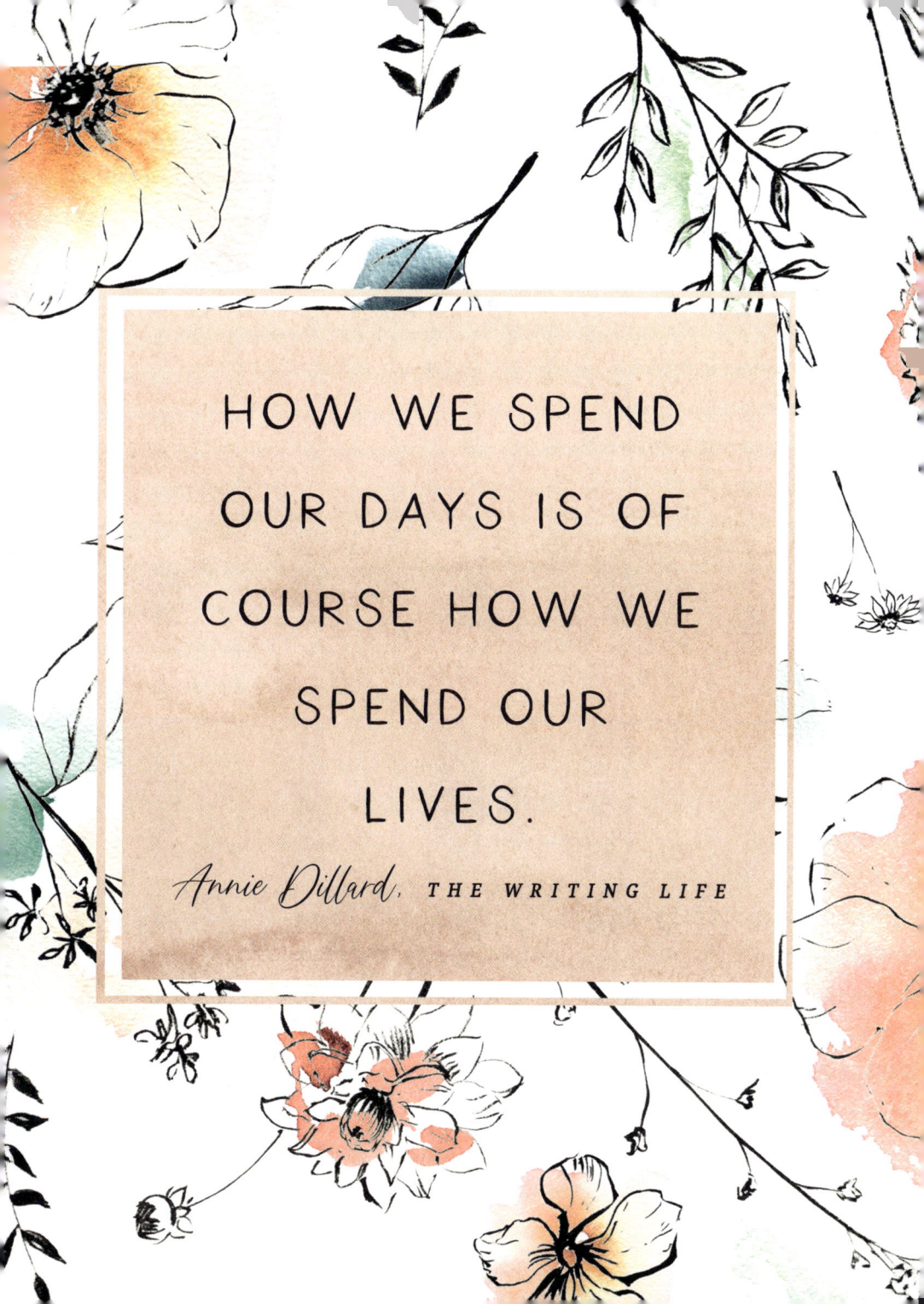

> HOW WE SPEND OUR DAYS IS OF COURSE HOW WE SPEND OUR LIVES.
>
> — *Annie Dillard*, THE WRITING LIFE

GIBBS SMITH
TO ENRICH AND INSPIRE HUMANKIND

First Edition
25 24 23 22 21   5 4 3 2 1

Text © 2021 Gibbs Smith Publisher
Illustrations © 2021 Sarah Cray
All rights reserved. No part of this book may be reproduced by any means whatsoever without written permission from the publisher, except brief portions quoted for purpose of review.

Published by
Gibbs Smith
P.O. Box 667
Layton, Utah 84041

1.800.835.4993 orders
www.gibbs-smith.com

Cover design by Sarah Cray
Printed and bound in China

Gibbs Smith books are printed on either recycled, 100% post-consumer waste, FSC-certified papers or on paper produced from sustainable PEFC-certified forest/controlled wood source. Learn more at www.pefc.org.

ISBN-13: 978-1-4236-5754-5